AN ALPHABET BOOK

IS FOR ORCA

PHOTOGRAPHS BY ART WOLFE
TEXT BY ANDREA HELMAN

SASQUATCH BOOKS

A is for auklet

The little auklet is a skillful swimmer. It dives into cold North Coast waters, propelling itself forward with narrow wings and steering with its feet.

B is for bear

A tiny black bear cub is born without teeth or fur, but it grows up to be a powerful adult. Each autumn, bears eat and eat so they can sleep through the long winter.

C is for coyote

Coyotes live and hunt together in family groups called packs. At night, they often howl together in a beautiful chorus.

D is for deer

The black-tailed deer fawn has a spotted coat that helps it hide in the forest.

E is for eagle

Bald eagles can fly up to 100 miles an hour! They roost in tall trees and swoop down to the water for a favorite meal of Pacific salmon.

F is for fir tree

The Douglas fir is shaped like a Christmas tree, with soft needles and a sweet fragrance. These trees can live for more than 750 years!

G is for goats

Mountain goats like steep and snowy alpine places. Just minutes after they're born, baby goats can stand and follow their mothers over rocky ground.

H is for Haida totem

The Haida people of the Queen Charlotte Islands in British Columbia are master carvers of totem poles, which record powerful family stories and legends of their people.

pole

I is for iceberg

In Alaska and the Yukon, icebergs form where glaciers meet the sea. Huge pieces of ice break off and float away on the frigid waters. Most of the iceberg is underwater!

J is for jay

In Northwest forests, the Steller's jay is one of the most colorful birds—and one of the loudest! They often visit backyard bird feeders.

K is for kelp

Bull kelp is one of the fastest-growing plants on earth. Hardy and long, this seaweed forms an underwater forest.

L is for lynx

The Canadian lynx is a shy, solitary cat that hunts at night in pine forests. It can run, but it really likes to climb trees.

M is for marmot

Marmots live in the mountains of the Pacific Northwest. They send high-pitched whistles to one another as a signal of approaching danger.

N is for Northern spotted owl

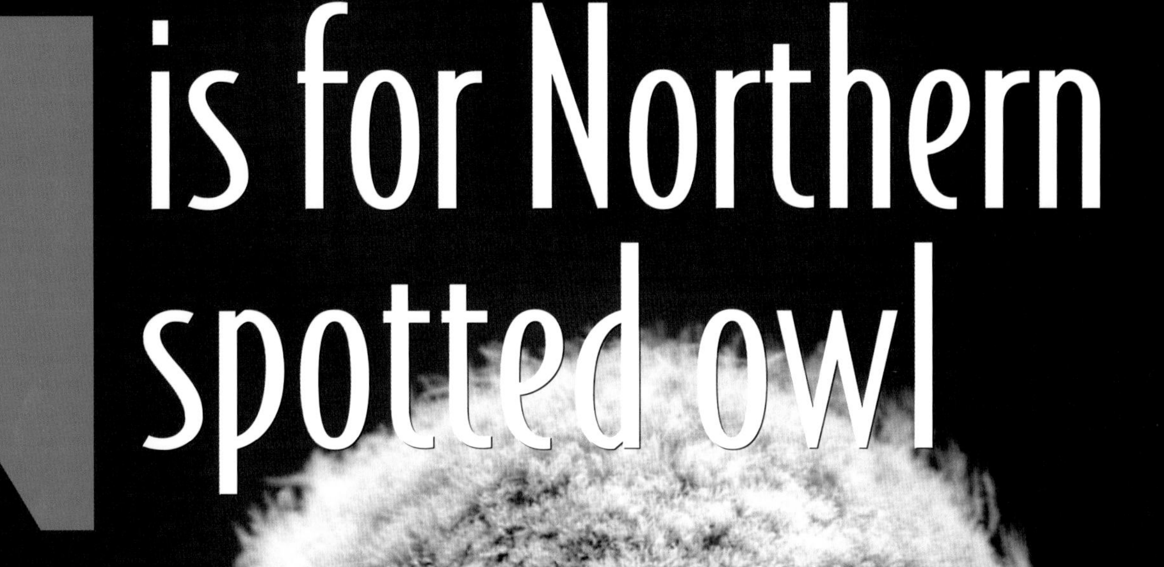

Northern spotted owls nest in old-growth forests along the Pacific Northwest coast. They are endangered because their natural habitat is disappearing.

O is for orca

Orcas are also called "killer whales," but they are friendly to people. Orcas live and travel in families, called pods, with the calves spending much of their lives alongside their mothers.

P is for puffin

The horned puffin lives along the coasts of Alaska and British Columbia. Its colorful beak can hold as many as thirty fish, or be used to give another puffin an affectionate peck!

Q is for quail

Quail fly only when threatened—otherwise they eat, sleep, and nest on the ground. Sometimes quail sit in a circle facing outward, keeping watch for unfriendly visitors.

R is for Mt. Rainier

Mount Rainier is actually a volcano! It is dormant now, but it could reawaken at any time.

S is for salmon

Salmon hatch in coastal rivers, then swim downstream to live in the sea. Years later they return to lay their eggs in their home rivers.

T is for tide pool

As the ocean tide goes out, it leaves pools of water among the rocks. These tide pools become separate little worlds, filled with sea stars, anemones, and urchins.

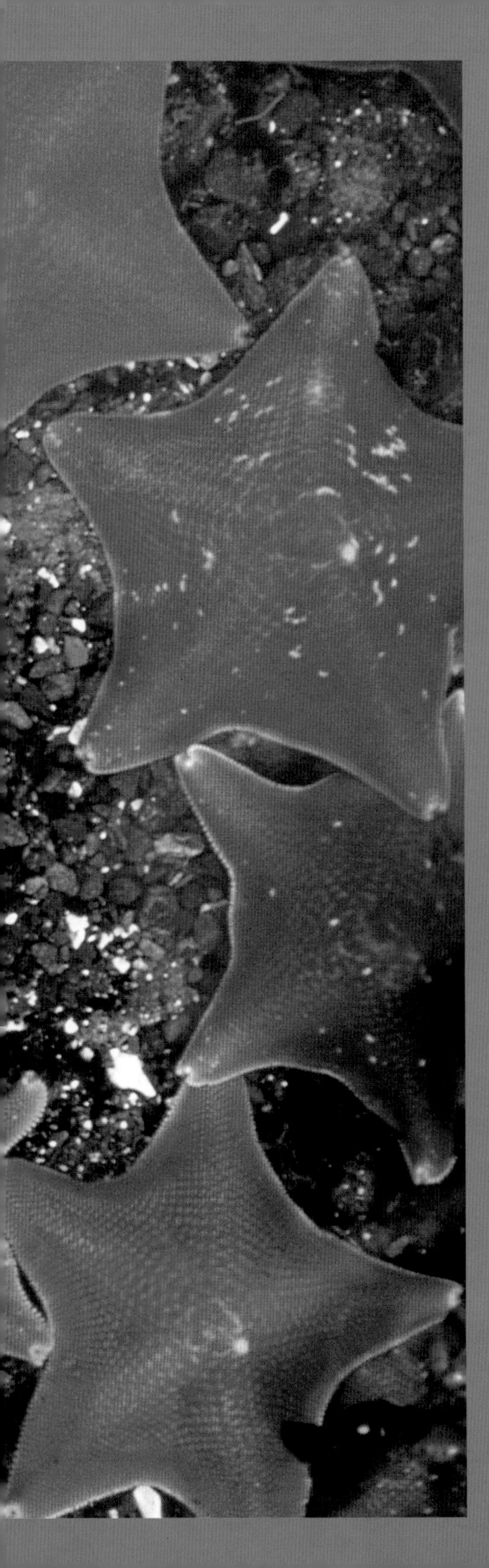

U is for urchin

Urchins cling to rocks in tide pools. The purple urchin has a hard outer covering of prickly spines, and sharp teeth for scraping food off rocks.

V is for volcano

The Pacific Northwest is a land of volcanoes. In 1980, Mount St. Helens, called the "fire mountain" by Native Americans, erupted in a violent explosion that blew off the entire mountaintop!

W is for wolf

The gray wolf is not a fast runner, but it can travel great distances. Wolves once roamed throughout the Pacific Northwest, but now they live mostly in Alaska and Canada.

X is for Xerophyllum tenax

The coarse blades of *Xerophyllum tenax* (the scientific name for "bear grass") were used by Native Americans to weave baskets that could hold and carry water.

Y is for Yakama

There are fourteen tribes in the Yakama confederation whose historic lands are located in south-central Washington State. They were known as great hunters and fishermen.

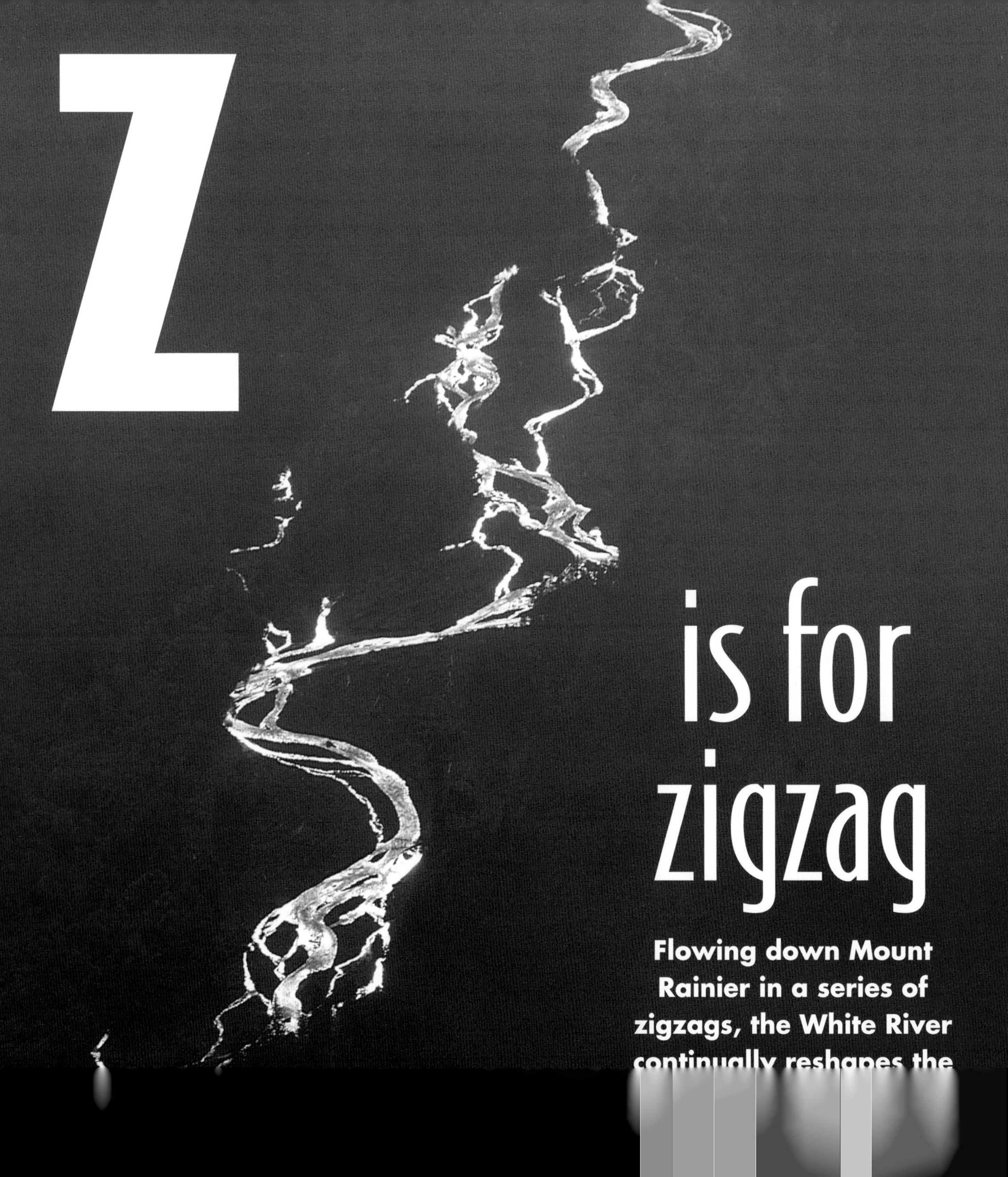

Z is for zigzag

Flowing down Mount Rainier in a series of zigzags, the White River continually reshapes the

Published by Sasquatch Books
Manufactured in China in February 2015 by Midas Printing International Ltd., NT, Hong Kong
Designed by Kate L. Thompson

Library of Congress Cataloging in Publication Data
Wolfe, Art.
O Is for Orca : an alphabet book / photographs by Art Wolfe ; text by
Andrea Helman.
p. cm.
ISBN 1-57061-038-X (hardcover) / ISBN 1-57061-392-3 (paperback)
1. Northwest, Pacific—Juvenile literature. 2. Alaska—Juvenile literature.
3. English language—Alphabet—Juvenile literature. [1. Northwest, Pacific.
2. Alaska. 3. Alphabet.] I. Helman, Andrea. II. Title.
F851.W76 1995
428.1—dc20 94-43908
[E]

1904 Third Avenue, Suite 710 Seattle,
WA 98101
(206) 467-4300
www.sasquatchbooks.com
custserv@sasquatchbooks.com